# Celebrity Pets
## Tell All

# Celebrity Pets Tell All

## Lai Ubberud

ATRIA BOOKS
New York London Toronto Sydney

BEYOND WORDS
PUBLISHING

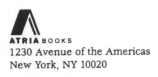

ATRIA BOOKS
1230 Avenue of the Americas
New York, NY 10020

BEYOND WORDS
PUBLISHING
20827 N.W. Cornell Road, Suite 500
Hillsboro, Oregon 97124-9808
503-531-8700 - 503-531-8773 fax
www.beyondword.com

Copyright © 2006 by Lai Ubberud

All rights reserved, including the right to reproduce this book
or portions thereof in any form whatsoever.

The information contained in this book is intended to be educational. The author
and publisher are in no way liable for any misuse of the information.

Editor: Jessica Bryan
Managing editor: Henry Covi
Cover, interior design, and composition: Jerry Soga
Illustrator: Jackie Somogyi

*Library of Congress Cataloging-in-Publication Data*
Ubberud, Lai.
    Celebrity pets tell all / by Lai Ubberud.
        p. cm.
    Includes bibliographical references.
1. Pets–Psychic aspects. 2. Extrasensory perception in animals. 3. Human-
animal communication. 4. Celebrities. I. Title.

    SF412.5.U23 2006
    636.088'7–dc22

                                                            2006022890

ISBN-13: 978-1-58270-155-4
ISBN-10:    1-58270-155-5

First Atria Books/Beyond Words trade paperback edition November 2006

10 9 8 7 6 5 4 3 2 1

**ATRIA** BOOKS is a trademark of Simon & Schuster, Inc.
Beyond Words Publishing is a division of Simon & Schuster, Inc.

Manufactured in the United States of America

For more information about special discounts for bulk purchases, please contact
Simon & Schuster Special Sales at 1-800-456-6798 or business@simonandschuster.com.

The corporate mission of Beyond Words Publishing, Inc.: *Inspire to Integrity*

This book is dedicated to my husband Lasse,
our children Anne-Kathrine, Frederick, and Madeleine, and
to all our pets, whether they've transitioned or are still
our companions in the physical.

# CONTENTS

## II. Do Famous Owners and Their Pets Get Together at the Rainbow Bridge?

## III. What Do Celebrity Pets Think About Their Coworkers?

## IV. How Do Celebrities Acquire Their Pets? Where Should Anyone Get a Pet?

## Pet Resources

# Can Animals Talk to People?

We always had pets when I was a child, and I loved to talk with them and hear what they had to say. I believed everybody could hear them and was surprised when my grandmother told me I had a special gift, and that not everyone could hear my beloved companions.

The family pets kept an eye on me and my sister—but especially me, because I was a tomboy who ended up getting in trouble quite often. My grandmother used to say: "Her guardian angels certainly keep an eye on her."

I also talked to wild animals. Their stories were quite different from our pets. They worried about hunters and predators, finding water, or having no food to eat. They worried about fires and being injured. They were concerned with the hot summers and the cold winters, and the safety of their babies. I felt sorry for them and wished I could help, but unfortunately there was nothing I could do except pray that none of their fears would come true.

When I was older, my husband and I traveled quite a bit, and I had the opportunity to meet all kinds of exotic animals. I often visited different zoos and had long talks with the myriad of species. Sometimes, I felt compassion for the animals who could not adjust to life in the zoo. They missed their freedom, and some of them missed their families because they had been caught but their loved ones had been left behind. Some of them told me they talked to migratory birds and asked them to give a message to their families if they happened to see them. Others became happy when the birds gave them news of their loved ones. It was quite exciting to talk with the animals in the zoo. One of my favorite places is the Krueger National Park in South Africa, where the animals roam free and there's no danger they will be captured and confined or killed by hunters.

Animals talk to me about their families and friends, their fears, joy, pain, favorite foods, the weather, and everything else—exactly like humans. What I wanted to accomplish by interacting with celebrity pets was to see the world from their perspective. Since all animals have emotions, desires, and intelligence—much the same way humans do—I knew these companion animals could offer readers a fresh look at their human friends. They could also offer us insight into the real people behind the façade of fame and fortune.

You, too, can communicate with your dog, cat, bird, or horse in the same way I tuned into these animals who live with celebrities. You can also talk with animals who are no longer in the physical. They don't speak words like we do, but rather they communicate telepathically, providing images and feelings that translate easily into intelligent communication. Each of us has this ability. Not only do our animal friends benefit from this kind of interaction, but a whole new world of possibilities can be opened up.

Sometimes, however, humans misunderstand their pets and end up having problems, independent of the particular kind of pet they have. The pet might tear up everything in sight, resist house-training, cower when touched, run away, and so forth. Quite often these people know very little about the pet they purchased. They may have bought the pet to give as a present, because it was fashionable, or perhaps they admired someone else who had a similar pet. What happens to animals in these situations? Most of the time, they're put in shelters or otherwise abandoned because their owners do not have the patience or interest necessary to do something about difficulties with a pet.

Some people know intuitively what animals are trying to communicate. They talk to them as if they are people, too. They understand animals and have an appreciation for what might be bothering an animal and how to help. Can they really "hear" what an animal is saying? I've lived with animals my entire life, and some of them seem more intelligent than others, which doesn't mean they're better trained. Actually, it's just the opposite: the more intelligent the pet, the more difficult training can become. Many people love their pets so much that their intuition tells them what the animal is saying. The pets recognize this and do their best to communicate what's on their minds.

People tell me quite often that they would like to have a pet, but there are all kinds of problems: it's too expensive; they have no time to care for a pet or no room in their home; or perhaps they fear animals. The decision to have a pet should always be considered carefully. Before making the decision to acquire a pet, try to find an animal that suits your particular situation. Sometimes it might only be a small aquarium with a few fish, but this is exactly what's needed. None of the people I've advised over the years have ever returned an animal or abandoned one.

What makes an animal happy? Is love, sufficient nutrition, and good care enough?

Is an animal with a diamond collar happier than one with a cheap collar from the local pet store?

What about food? Is a cat who eats caviar healthier or happier than a cat who eats regular cat food?

Is a pet living in a wealthy household less afraid of loud noises than an alley cat?

Finally, does a pet who belongs to someone who is rich and famous love his or her owner more than a pet who belongs to the average person?

Well, this is what we're going to find out. In the following chapters, I'll share with you what some pets really think about their celebrity owners, and also what some celebrity pets who are famous for their own work think about the actors and actresses they work with.

—Lai Ubberud

# ACKNOWLEDGEMENTS

I would like to thank my friend Krys Goclowski for her help and support and my friend Bridget O'Brien, who believed in the possible and inspired me to bring it forth.

# I

# Some Famous Owners and Their Pets

# Paris Hilton & Tinkerbell

Occasionally, I see news about Paris Hilton on television. Generally speaking, the commentators are sarcastic about her wild ideas. I never paid too much attention, until "Tinkerbell," her dog, got lost. Then I started wondering: Was she completely indifferent to her dog, or was it just a freak accident? I couldn't resist investigating the relationship between Paris and Tinkerbell, so as soon as I could I sat down with their photo and meditated on them.

Tinkerbell is a wise dog, and she knows Paris better than anybody else, even better than Paris knows herself. I asked her if she would talk to me about Paris, but she was worried I was going to trash her like some of the reporters. I promised her I wouldn't. She seemed rather relieved and told me she trusted me enough to talk about Paris:

**"Paris is a bit spoiled and gets bored easily. When she's bored she doesn't consider the consequences of her actions. She has a lot of imagination and is very intelligent. But, unfortunately, she's not yet mature enough to use her creativity wisely."**

I was impressed with Tinkerbell's analysis of Paris because that was exactly what I was thinking. Then I asked her if it was really true that Paris had lost her.

**Tinkerbell became serious: "No, she didn't lose me; she only forgot to bring me home. I'm not sure if she did it on purpose to call attention to herself or if it was a freak accident. She's affectionate, but sometimes she has a short attention span. She moves from one project to another without thinking them through."**

"What do you think about her other animals?" I said.

**She looked away for a moment and then said: "They're alright, but I don't care too much for them—except Bambi."**

"I understand," I said. "But what do the other pets think about Paris?"

**"They agree entirely with me. We're lucky we belong to someone who feeds us, gives us a good home, and takes care of us—instead of being homeless, hungry, and scared."**

Somehow I knew Tinkerbell wouldn't tell me anything else, so I thanked her and said good-by.

# Philip Treacy & Mr. Pig

I started noticing Philip Treacy a few years ago when I was glancing through fashion magazines. He was making hats for the British Royal Family, other European Royals, and socialites. I thought he was very brave because not many people wear hats these days. I was intrigued and wondered why he decided to start making hats. Where did he get his inspiration? I had cut a photo of him with his dog, "Mr. Pig," out of a magazine a few months earlier, and I decided to study it.

Mr. Pig is a happy and playful dog with a British sense of humor. He enjoys talking about his owner, whom he calls "Master Philip." Mr. Pig must have enormous respect for him or he wouldn't call him "Master." I asked Mr. Pig to tell me something about Master Philip because I wanted to find out more about Philip's creative inspiration.

**"Well," he said, "Master Philip started making clothes and hats for dollies when he was only five years old."**

I was really impressed with this, especially since my sewing skills are limited. I asked him: "Where did Master Philip find the materials to make the doll clothes?"

**"Oh, he grew up on a farm in Ireland, and his parents had geese, ducks, and chickens. He used to pick up the feathers and sew them onto the clothes and hats," said Mr. Pig.**

*What a smart little boy,* I thought.

**"He went through school, and as he grew up his interest in fashion increased. He graduated with honors from the university and then went to work for a big designer."**

I asked him which designer and he replied, **"Karl something.... I can't remember."**

**"Now, Master Philip has his own boutique," he told me proudly. "It's a lot of responsibility, but I'm there to help him."**

Obviously, Mr. Pig is very sure of himself.

"Okay," I said. "Now that you've told me about Master Philip's achievements, please tell me what it's like to be with him."

"Well," said Mr. Pig, with a smug smile on his face, "He has skinny legs."

I burst into laughter at this comment. Why would a dog want to comment on someone's legs?

Mr. Pig went on: "He likes to play ball with me, and sometimes we fall asleep together on the settee. Master Philip tells me all about his designs, and I always give my opinion. I definitely let him know when I don't like something. I also send him telepathic messages, and he uses them, even though he believes the ideas are his own. I really don't know how he would survive without me."

I thanked Mr. Pig for his insight. He had been extremely helpful and a lot of fun to talk to.

# Buzz Aldrin,
# Tiber & Luna

When my son was little he wanted to go to the moon. He loved watching the first two Americans who landed on the moon. He asked a lot of questions, and we were able to answer most of them. Every time I saw a magazine about space shuttles I would buy it for him. In the meantime, he changed his mind and decided he wanted to go to Mars instead!

I was going through some old magazines and found one with an article about the second man who landed on the moon. It brought back memories, so I decided to look him up on the Internet. I found a photo of Buzz Aldrin with his two cats. Unfortunately, I didn't print it out, but I did look at it long enough to be able to communicate with the cats. I scribbled down what they told me and then put the paper away and forgot about it—until I started writing this book.

I found the paper again rather easily, which I took as a sign that I was supposed to write about those cats and their famous owner. Now, I only had to make sure I could read what I had written. I couldn't believe my handwriting was so messy. I said to myself: *I should have been a doctor; the pharmacist would have been able to help me. But since I'm not a doctor, I'd better start deciphering my own hieroglyphs.*

This is what I had written: "Buzz Aldrin was the second man on the moon. He's tall, fit, and a true astronaut. He must be pretty tough to go so far away. Going to the moon is not the same as flying somewhere on earth, even if the flight is to the other side of the world."

I wondered: *Just because this man is tough, is he insensitive or does he have a soft side that we don't know about? Well, his cats can help me find out.* First, I asked them to tell me their names.

**"I'm Luna," said one of them.**

**"And I'm Tiber," said the other one.**

"What beautiful names. I know 'Luna' means 'moon,' but what does 'Tiber' mean?"

**"Tiber is the moon of a planet that Buzz invented for a novel, but I like it," said the beautiful cat.**

"Please tell me about Buzz." I said.

"In spite of his tough looks, he's a sweetheart and loves cuddling us. He also likes talking to us," said Luna.

"Buzz is intelligent and really enjoyed being an astronaut. He's also a pilot and has done a lot of other things. He wrote a book; he was on television; and there was even a film about him. He was angry and sad when he found out his watch had been stolen," Tiber said.

"We also love the rest of the family. They treat us so well. We're lucky to have such a nice family," said Luna. "Of course, we have known Buzz for many reincarnations. We were already together in Egypt, when we lived there 4,000 years ago."

"What were you in that life?" I said.

"We were cats then, too. We've taken the bodies of different animals, but we like being cats the best."

I thanked these two cats, who had so much personality. I was also happy to learn more about the second man on the moon.

# Hilary Duff & Little Dog

I usually read popular magazines when I go to the doctor, dentist, or hairdresser. One day, I was browsing through a magazine while waiting for my doctor, when I saw a photo of a little mutt with a beautiful blond girl. When I looked into his eyes, I felt he had suffered a lot, but he was now a happy dog. I started reading the article and found out that the blond girl was none other than Hilary Duff, the teenage singer and actress.

I had only heard nice things about this young woman, but was she as good as people said, or was there something hidden behind that engaging smile? I was curious, so as soon as my appointment with the doctor was over, I went downstairs and bought my very own copy of the magazine. I absolutely had to take the photo home to concentrate on it.

As soon as I could, I started meditating on the mutt. His name was "Little Dog," and he was a serious dog, one who only spoke when spoken to. I asked him to please tell me about himself, Hilary, and her family. His eyes softened, and I noticed a couple of grateful tears in his eyes.

He told me he had been abandoned by his first owner. At the time, he didn't know that pets could be dropped off in shelters, so he thought his owner didn't like him anymore.

**"Now I know that if a person cannot keep a pet, he can take it to a shelter. But it's still difficult for me to forgive, and it's even harder to forget. After all, I'm a Scorpio," he said**

I understood him very well because I'm also a Scorpio.

**He continued: "I was hungry, cold, and scared. Honestly, I thought my days would end pretty soon unless a miracle happened."**

I was sorry to hear that he had suffered so much, but I firmly believed Hilary had made up for the horrors he had been through.

Little Dog smiled and said that he had been guided by his grandmother—who was in heaven—to go and scratch on the back door of a little girl who was sad because her first dog had died. His grandmother told him the little girl would take good care of him and that her whole family would love him forever.

I was impressed by the fact that Little Dog's grandmother was also his "Guardian Dog." She must have suffered terribly as she watched him get lost and become thirsty, cold, and disoriented. I asked him: "Is Hilary as sweet and good as they say?"

**"Oh yes," he replied. "She's the nicest teenager on earth, and she has lots of common sense, too. She's also compassionate and gives a lot of money to charity."**

I had heard this on television, so it was no surprise.

**Little Dog continued: "I sleep on her bed, but she's always busy and doesn't have enough time to sleep as much as she would like to." Then he added: "She's very intelligent, and I'm sure she'll do well in college."**

That was all I could get out of him, but I had the most important information: Hilary is as nice a person as the magazine said.

# George Clooney & Max

Who hasn't heard of George Clooney, that gorgeous hunk who has played in so many action films and the television series *ER*? Not only is he a great actor, but he's also goodlooking. Why hasn't he met his soul mate and settled down? There must be somebody out there for him. What kind of person is he, really? Is he merely a Casanova out for conquests or is he just an ordinary man who enjoys feminine company in small portions? Is he too settled in his ways to even consider a lifetime partner?

Well there's only one way to find out: talk to his beloved companion of many years, "Max" the pig!

Max is an extremely intelligent pot-bellied pig, who worships the ground his human companion walks on. He would *never* consider George Clooney to be his master or owner—they're partners in every way. After all, they've been through so much together.

I asked Max what he calls George Clooney.

**"Why, 'George,' of course. What else would I call him? He's my roommate, not my boss," said Max.**

*Okay,* I thought. *Here is a pig with a strong personality. I'd better ask the questions carefully or he won't tell me anything.*

I asked Max to tell me something about himself. He liked that and started talking immediately.

**"I came to George's house many years ago when I was only a piglet. He had a girlfriend at the time. Unfortunately, they broke up."**

As he was telling me this, Max rolled his eyes. I almost burst into laughter, but I managed to keep a serious face. I was afraid of antagonizing him and not hearing his story.

**Max went on: "I was afraid I might need to go and live with the girlfriend, Kelly, because sometimes women go crazy and decide to dress their male pigs in feminine clothes. I wouldn't like that at all! Fortunately, I was able to stay with George, and we're good buddies."**

"What's George like, really, not as a movie star but as a man?" I said.

"George has quite a strong personality, and he's settled in his ways. He works hard and has a great sense of humor. Even though he enjoys dressing up and going to parties, he also likes wearing jeans or his swimming trunks and just lying around playing with the dogs or watching a game."

He continued: "George also became wiser about my food. He doesn't starve me, but he doesn't let me eat as much as he used to. I get annoyed sometimes because I really like my food, but I finally accepted the fact that I'm a mature pig now and don't need as much food as I did when I was younger. Oh well, those were the days," said Max.

He seemed a bit nostalgic for the larger meals of the past.

"George was shaken up when his Aunt Rosemary died, and it took him a while to get over it. He is quite attached to his family," said Max.

"How did you feel about the two new dogs moving in?" I said.

"Oh, they were a bit of a nuisance to start with because they were not house-trained," he said in disgust. "They barked all the time and left their toys all over the place, so we had to be careful and watch where we stepped. Fortunately, they're house-trained now and also more settled, so they don't bother me. They used to start barking as soon as I fell asleep."

Obviously, Max's beauty sleep is important to him.

"Speaking of sleep, why aren't you allowed to sleep with George?" I said.

Max had a half-annoyed, smug smile on his face. "George thinks I take up too much space and I snore."

"Is it true? Do you snore?"

"Don't be silly. How would I know? I can't hear myself when I'm asleep," he said.

There was a somewhat frustrated look on his face. Even though Max didn't say so, I could see he was starting to have a few doubts about my intelligence.

I questioned him further: "I need to know what's going on with George and the women in his life. Should he find a life partner to love and who will love him?"

Max thought for a moment and then said: "I hope he meets the woman of his dreams pretty soon, but George is so picky. We're going to need a miracle here. I've been telling him for a few years to start looking, but he won't listen. I won't be able to take care of him forever."

Max is a sensible and helpful animal. I thanked him for his cooperation and wished him good luck in finding the ideal woman for George.

# Britney Spears & Bit Bit

A few months ago, one of my teenage clients, who is an animal lover, said: "Did you know Britney Spears has another dog?"

I told her I didn't know Britney had any dogs. I only knew she had a baby boy.

"Oh yeah, I know about the baby, but the dogs are so cute," she said.

Obviously, she was more interested in the dogs than the baby.

She asked me if I knew what the dogs thought about their owner, and I told her that when I had time I would look into it. She was excited about this and kept sending me e-mails reminding me of my promise. She's a good girl, so I decided to sit down and find out about Britney and her new dog.

"Bit Bit" is a shy, tiny Chihuahua who has been with Britney Spears for awhile. It took some convincing to get any information out of him. "I'm not interested in gossip such as who she sleeps with or anything like that," I told him. "I just want to find out what kind of person she is. After all, she's so famous but so young. It must be hard for her."

**Bit Bit warmed to the subject: "Oh yes. It's hard because we can't go to the mall with our friends and hang out without the paparazzi following us everywhere. If she makes even the smallest mistake her picture is splashed all over the tabloids. When she was younger, she cried when she was criticized. She never knew when she might be watched, and even when she met somebody she liked, she couldn't be sure if they were only trying to become her friend because she was famous. It's really tough on a kid."**

"What happened to her first marriage and why was there an annulment?" I said.

**"I think it was a publicity stunt, and she got cold feet, so she wanted to get out of it as soon as she could."**

**He went on without further prompting: "I'm happy to have**

Lucky [Britney's other dog]. It's company, you know? I was pretty lonely before, because Britney works so much. We have our own bedroom and a little brother. We can't wait until he's big enough to play with us. We're really lucky to have such a great life."

# Tori Spelling & Mimi

I've always considered Tori Spelling to be a down-to-earth woman, in spite of being the daughter of a genius like Aaron Spelling. The first time I went to Los Angeles, I took a bus tour with my family and, sure enough, we stopped to look at their house. We were impressed with its size, but I didn't think too much about it.

At the time, *Beverly Hills 90210* was airing. The show was popular, and I always liked Tori in her role as Donna Martin. She seemed to be a nice young woman. I wondered if she was just as nice in real life or whether she was only acting.

I really wanted to know, so I decided to sit down and concentrate on a photo of her with her pug, "Mimi," who is a shy little dog who measures her words carefully. Mimi said she trusted me and would answer my questions about Tori. I was delighted, but before I could ask my first question, Mimi started talking:

**"There was a vet who thought I was dim-witted, but he was completely wrong. I'm not dim-witted at all. I'm an old soul and have lived many times. I enjoy observing people and the world around me. I also meditate a lot. Some people think you need to run around like a maniac to be productive. I disagree. Everybody needs time to sit down and look inside. Tori thinks she chose me, but it was me who chose her. We have had many lives together, and I wanted to be with her again in this lifetime."**

I was absolutely impressed with the wisdom and knowledge of this dog. What a philosopher. This promised to be a very interesting conversation, so I said: "Tell me about the first time you saw Tori."

**Mimi smiled. "Tori came into the pet store to get a male dog, like her boyfriend wanted, but when she saw me, she picked me up and that was it. Of course, she wasn't aware that I was sending her telepathic messages about our past lives together and that she absolutely needed to take me so we could continue our relationship. Actually, all of the animals she has now have also had one or more past lives with her. We love her so much that we wanted to come back and be with her again."**

Mimi continued: "Tori is a nice young woman with a lot of common sense. She's not spoiled at all, in spite of being the daughter of such an important man. Tori is compassionate and loves animals. She didn't know that animals could be rescued from shelters. When she found out, she never went back to a pet store except to buy food and things for us. She also does a lot of charity work for pets."

I had already heard about this, so I knew Mimi had the facts straight.

"I was sick for a while. Tori took me to see several vets, but they couldn't treat me. Then she heard about a holistic doctor and took me there. I was scared when I found out they would be sticking needles in me, but it wasn't so bad. I feel much better now."

"What about the other animals Tori has adopted?" I said.

"They're okay. Each of us has our own territory. I was quite happy to meet Leah, but I knew she wasn't the little angel she pretended to be, and was I right."

"What did Leah do?" I said.

"She pulled out the toilet paper from the bathrooms, chewed on Tori's stuffed animals, and peed on the floor. It was disgusting. She's lucky because Tori just laughed about it. But I was afraid Tori would think I had done it," Mimi said, looking rather relieved.

I laughed at the thought of having toilet paper all over our apartment, because one of our cats did that, too.

# Martha Stewart & Paw Paw

Who hasn't heard of Martha Stewart, the talented woman who made housekeeping, cooking, and baking an honorable avocation? I admire her work and know-how. She's a walking housekeeping encyclopedia. I like to watch her show when I have time to spare. I really admire the way she makes everything look so simple: decorations, cooking, and baking. My favorite shows are the ones during which she demonstrates cooking. I also like the shows when she brings her pets. She has so many, and they're all so lovely.

I began to wonder: She has a big house with enough space for them, but how do her pets feel about Martha? Do they get along or do they resent each other? Do they compete for her attention? Do they feel left out sometimes? And, what about the chickens? Do the dogs and cats chase them or do they feel safe?

I would think about these things and then something would happen and I would forget about them completely, until the next time I saw her on television or came across her magazine.

One day, I bought a magazine and there it was: a photo of Martha Stewart with one of her chows. At last, I had something to work with. I definitely wanted to take the time to have a talk with this adorable chow chow, who is named "Paw Paw." What an appropriate name for such a beautiful dog! I concentrated on the photo and asked Paw Paw if he would talk with me.

**He looked as if he was judging me, and then he said seriously: "Yes, I will. You're an animal lover so maybe you can help me straighten out a few things. I've tried to explain to people about Martha, but they can't hear me. I also had some pet psychics ask me questions, but I didn't answer because they were not sincere or honest. It's rather frustrating, but I like your energy and you can hear me, so let's have a talk."**

I was flattered by his knowledge of psychology. *What a smart dog, and what a good judge of character*, I thought.

"What is Martha Stewart really like? Some magazines describe her as a cold person," I said.

**"What do you think?" he responded.**

"I think they're wrong. Martha is a private person. I know she's always on television, but I also wonder if she's a little shy and doesn't like to show affection in public."

**Grinning, he said: "You're absolutely right. When she's with her family, friends, and pets, she's completely different: open, affectionate, and funny. It's rather difficult to be always in the limelight and know that any little mistake you make will be criticized publicly and turned into a major disaster."**

"I can certainly understand that," I said.

**"She's intelligent and good at everything she does. She's also rather humble," said Paw Paw.**

Obviously he knew Martha better than anybody else, so I believed him. "What about the other animals? Do you like them, too?" I said.

**"I love the dogs. We're all good friends. I don't care too much for the cats, because they think they're better than us. They're so full of themselves."**

Of course, I believed him because he sounded so disgusted. "What about the birds, the chinchillas, and the chickens?" I said.

**"Well, I like to listen to the canaries, and I don't mind the chinchillas, but the chickens can get quite noisy, especially after they've laid an egg. They make such a fuss about it. They don't seem to understand that it's their job: laying eggs so Martha**

can use them for cooking and baking. I've tried to tell them this, over and over, but it doesn't work. Every time I close my eyes to take a nap, they start their little concert."

Paw Paw had made it perfectly clear that he wasn't amused by the noisy chickens, because they interrupted his beauty sleep.

"Martha is busy with her work and has so many pets. Does she have enough time for all of you?" I said.

"Oh yes. I don't know how she does it, but she finds time for each of her pets. We all feel much loved, but we do worry about her working too hard."

"I read somewhere that you competed in the Westminster show. Did you enjoy being in such a prestigious competition?"

"I enjoyed it immensely," said Paw Paw. "Even though I didn't win, I had a lot of fun and made a lot of new friends. I wish I could have won for Martha, but she knew I had done my best. She wasn't upset or anything, just a little disappointed, but so was I."

I assured him I knew exactly what he meant, because we had taken one of our dogs to some shows.

"Now, I have a rather delicate question. How did you feel when Martha was in trouble and had to spend some time in jail?" I said, as casually as I could.

"The whole thing was completely crazy, but the worst part was being separated from Martha for such a long time, and we were not even sure if she was okay. All her pets missed her terribly," he said. "It was a sad day when she had to leave us behind."

I could see the sadness in his eyes and felt sorry for him and Martha's other pets.

I thanked him for his cooperation and said good-by.

# Ivana Trump, Choppy & Dodo

Many years ago, I read an article about a beautiful young skier from Czechoslovakia who had met a rich American. They fell in love, got married, and expected to "live happily ever after." What a lovely story. I hoped someone would make a film about them.

Their names were Ivana and Donald Trump.

I would see their photos in the fashion magazines from

time to time and, as expected, they had children. But then Ivana and Donald got divorced. *Oh, well, it can happen to anybody, but it's a pity because there are children involved*, I thought.

Then I started seeing photos of Ivana that had been taken at social functions. Honestly, I didn't pay too much attention to her until I saw her in a photo with two adorable tiny dogs. *That's my kind of person*, I thought. *Perhaps she just loves animals.* I wondered whether she really loved the dogs or whether it was just a show for the tabloids.

I bought the magazine and found out she works with an animal rescue association. *What a great person*, I thought. *All that money and she still finds time to help animals.*

Needless to say, I became curious and decided to have a talk with her two adorable pooches, who seemed rather mischievous. "What are your names?" I said.

They looked at me as if they expected me to already know the answer to my own question, so I told them their names were not given in the magazine and that they hadn't said a word to me, yet.

**They both giggled and then one of them said, "Oops, sorry. I'm 'Choppy' and that's 'Dodo.' What's your name?"**

"My name is 'Lai,' and I love animals. May I ask you a few questions about your life and family?"

**"Sure," they said at the same time. "What do you want to know?"**

I began to wonder whether they would tell me the truth or whether they would make up a story just to play a trick on me. I'd better keep my eyes open—they were little clowns who got bored easily and enjoyed playing tricks on people. I decided to tell them that I would appreciate their giving me the truth and not making up stories.

**They looked at each other and said: "Oh, oh."**

They seemed disappointed that I had found out what they were up to so quickly. When they started talking, they completed each other sentences. I could tell they were definitely using telepathy because they were so bonded.

"What's it like to live with Ivana?" I said.

**"It's great. She dotes on us and treats us very well. Ivana takes us everywhere." This comment produced more giggles.**

"I don't believe you," I said.

**They were taken aback by my remark, and looking guilty, one of them said: "You're right. She can't take us everywhere because she travels a lot. We really miss her when she's not with us."**

"Now you're talking. Thank you for being honest."

**"We'll try," they said. "She's always quite busy but enjoys her work. She's also smart and never feels sorry for herself. She can always find a solution."**

"What about the children?" I asked.

**"They're okay. One girl, Ivanka, is a model and the others go to**

school. Ivana loves them very much and so do we."

"Do you know if Ivana is over the divorce?" I asked.

"She was hurt, angry, and disappointed. She cried a lot, but now she's fine. She's beautiful and caring, and a lot of men fall in love with her."

"What do you think about Donald Trump?" I said.

"He's okay, but he really needs a good haircut! We don't understand why he doesn't do it. We're sure he has enough money to go to a better hairdresser."

I laughed at their comments.

Choppy and Dodo continued: "She helps at one of the animal shelters. What's it called?" They looked at each other as if they expected the other would remember the name of the shelter.

"I know the name," I said. "It's 'The North Shore Animal League.' That's why I contacted you. I was never too interested in her life until I saw an article about the League that mentioned her."

"That's right!" they exclaimed in unison.

They winked at me, and I knew they wouldn't tell me anything else.

# Carol Burnett & Roxy

When I was growing up, I always tried to watch *The Carol Burnett Show*. The whole family loved it. We laughed at her performances and decided to elect her "The Queen of Comedy." As I got older, I didn't have much time to watch television and only remembered her when I read something in a magazine. Then memories of old episodes would come back.

One day, I was glancing at a magazine in a market while

waiting to pay for my groceries. I noticed an article about Carol Burnett that included a photo of her with a cat. I immediately put the magazine in the cart and brought it home so I could read the entire article.

As soon as I had some free time, I sat down to read. I couldn't take my eyes off the photo. It was almost as if the cat wanted my attention. I gave up and decided to talk to the cat first. I could always read the article later. Obviously, "Roxy" didn't want to take second place! She wanted me to listen to her straight away. The article about Carol had to wait.

"Okay," I said. "Since you won't let me read, you'd better start talking. I'm all ears."

**"I couldn't wait to meet somebody who could hear me," said Roxy. She sounded quite relieved. "I've been with Carol for a few years, and I don't know what she would do without me. She doesn't remember it, but we've been together in other lives. I always took care of her when I was alive, and when my body died my spirit came back to be with her and guide her."**

"I believe you," I said. "A lot of the pets I've interviewed say the same thing—they were with their owners in other lives."

**Roxy continued: "Carol was born in San Antonio, but she left Texas when she was young. She was brought up by her grandmother. It was hard for Carol when her grandmother passed away."**

"Please tell me about her career," I said.

"She's a great actress, hardworking, and she takes her work seriously. She's a simple person, in spite of being so famous. I just wish she wouldn't travel so much. She gets tired sometimes, and so do I. She was the winner of the 2003 Kennedy Center Honors Award. I'm very proud of her."

"Did you know she got angry at one of the tabloids and sued them?" Roxy added.

"No, did she win?"

Roxy looked at me as if she thought something was wrong with me. She blurted out: "Of course, she did! It wasn't for the money; It was the principle."

"I can understand that," I reassured her. I really didn't want Roxy to get mad at me.

"Unfortunately, Carol has been through so much," said Roxy. "The worst was the death of her daughter Carrie when the child was still so young. It was horrible. Carol tried to be strong for Carrie, but it was pretty hard. We both cried a lot. Carrie is with us in spirit now, and I talk to her all the time. It's a pity Carol can't see or hear her because it would make her feel better."

Roxy went on: "I'm so happy Carol found love again. She deserves it. Thank you so much for listening to me. I really needed to get a few things off my chest."

She waved her paw at me, and I began to read the magazine article about Carol Burnett.

# Mary Tyler Moore, Shana & Shadow

Mary Tyler Moore was one of the first women to be in a television series, and she has never stopped acting. She's a living legend and has won many awards. There's even a statue of her in Minneapolis. I've never heard anybody criticize her. I've only heard nice things about her.

I read somewhere that she has diabetes and wondered about her health. What about the death of her only son? How did she cope with it? Did she feel any responsibility for his death? Is she over it by now? Is she a true animal lover or is it all about publicity? I became intrigued by this formidable woman, who has brought so much laughter to so many people, but whose life has been personally troubled.

I found a photo of Mary Tyler Moore with her pooches: "Shana," a schnauzer, and "Shadow," a golden retriever. I asked them to please tell me something about their life with Mary. They immediately agreed. Shadow was reserved, but Shana was bubbly and began talking straight away.

**"My name is 'Shana Meydela.' It means 'Pretty Girl.' I really love my name because it suits me," she said.**

Shadow shook his head as if he was bored. He must have heard this many times before and obviously thought she was rather vain.

"Everyone knows Mary is a great actress. Would you please comment on her brilliant career?" I said.

**Shana was quite emphatic: "She has won many prizes, and there's even a statue of her someplace, but I can't remember the name."**

**"Minneapolis," Shadow interrupted.**

"I'm going to Minneapolis soon. I'll try to see it," I said.

They both looked at me and smiled. Obviously, they were happy to hear that I was planning to pay tribute to their beloved Mary.

"How is her health? I heard she has diabetes." I said.

They looked at each other, concern on their faces. Shadow spoke: "Mary is doing better now. She doesn't see very well and had problems with one of her legs. Fortunately, her husband is a doctor and takes good care of her."

"I'm happy to hear that. She's such a lovely person," I said. "What about the death of her son? Is she over it?"

Again, it was Shadow who answered: "It was terrible, and even though she learned to cope, it still hurts. And it's not only Richie's death. There have been many other deaths in the family. One of her sisters committed suicide; another one died of cancer; and her mother also passed away. It has been a lot for her, poor thing."

My heart went out to this brave woman. Shana and I had tears in our eyes as we thought about how much Mary has suffered the last few years. I just hope that from now on only good things will happen to her.

I didn't want to bring up any more bad memories for these two lovely pets, so I changed the subject: "Tell me about her work with animal rescue."

They both started talking at the same time. I couldn't understand anything they said and had to ask them to please take turns.

Shadow spoke first: "Mary really loves animals and wants to protect us. She has even been to the government to defend us. Money is very important in the human world, so she organizes all kinds of events to raise money for animals and..."

"Did you know she doesn't use any animal products? She's also a vegetarian," Shana interrupted.

Shadow frowned and then continued: "As I was saying when I was so rudely interrupted, she uses her influence to convince scientists not to use animals for experiments."

"Does Mary have any other pets besides the two of you?"

"Oh yes. She has horses and goats, but no cats. She isn't a cat person, fortunately. I don't care for cats, myself," said Shadow. "Mary's other animals live on a farm, and we love going there to visit. They also love to see us. We're all really good friends."

"I don't care for cats, either," said Shana. "By the way, I'm the reincarnation of her first dog, a cocker spaniel. My name used to be 'Wendy' in that life, but I like my new name better."

I thanked them both for their help and threw them a kiss. These dogs were as nice as Mary Tyler Moore, their human companion.

# Jason Priestly & Swifty

As soon as the television show *Beverly Hills 90210* started, it became a big hit. My friends opinions were divided about the character Brandon Walsh, who was played by Jason Priestly. Some people thought Brandon was boring; others absolutely loved him. I liked his integrity and honesty. Perhaps he wasn't the most exciting person in the series, but he made it look more real, and he had good morals.

The series ended, but occasionally I would see news stories about the various actors and actresses. When I was writing this book, I saw a photo of Jason Priestly and his dog

"Swifty." I knew immediately that I wanted to hear what this lovely French bulldog had to say about his adoptive Canadian father. I concentrated on the photo and felt that Swifty was full of mischief and was a little spoiled, but adorable.

"Would you mind answering some questions?" I said.

**"I was planning to take a nap. Can it wait?" said Swifty.**

"I guess so," I said, rather startled.

**"Good, talk to you later," he said as he closed his eyes.**

I knew I wouldn't get any immediate answers and would need to wait until he woke up.

About 45 minutes later, when he woke up from his snooze, he was in a much better mood.

**"So, what's this about?" he said.**

"I'm writing a book about celebrities and their pets, and I would like to write about you and Jason."

**"Of course you would. We are important celebrities. You can't have a book about celebrities and their pets and not put me in it!" he said. "What guarantee do you have that I won't tell you a pack of lies?"**

*This is not going to be easy,* I thought. But I wasn't going to let him intimidate me. "I'm pretty good at detecting lies, and I don't see what you have to gain by misleading me. I won't trash either you or Jason; I promise."

He calmed down a little, so then I asked, "Who is the boss, you or Jason?"

**"That would be me, of course. He really spoils me and I love it."**

I noticed he had a twinkle in his eye. "Are you lonely when you can't be with him?" I said.

**"Oh, yes. It gets pretty lonely when he's not around."**

I decided to change the subject before he decided to take another nap. "So what do you think about his career? Are you proud of him?"

**"He's a great actor, and working with Edie Falco was a great experience for him. He also produced and directed some episodes of Beverly Hills 90210. He's quite gifted."**

Swifty's pride in Jason was quite evident.

"What about racing?" I said.

**He rolled his eyes. "What a nightmare. I'm always worried about him, especially since his big accident, but he is not an aggressive driver anymore. He's more mature."**

"That's a relief. Now, can you tell me something about his love life?" I said, hoping he wouldn't play a fast one on me.

**"Ashlee and Jason got divorced, and he married Naomi last year. I was happy for him because he's been lonely, in spite of my company. I hope they have a baby so I can play with it and take care of it," he said, and then added: "He's very particular**

about his hair, but I love it. It really suits him."

He seemed rather puzzled when I burst into laughter. He definitely didn't understand what was so funny. I decided to ask another question before he got annoyed. "Please tell me about the shelter called 'Much Love Animal Rescue.'" I said.

He responded with enthusiasm: "It's a great organization. Lots of celebrities go there and bring their dogs. I love the parties. Do you have any more questions? I'm starting to get tired again. I need another nap."

I thanked him for his help, but he had the last word.

"Are you sure I told you the truth?"

I just laughed and threw him a kiss.

# Shania Twain & Tim

Who hasn't heard of Shania Twain? She's so beautiful and successful, and she's in the news all the time. Occasionally, I read articles about her that are not so flattering, and I wonder whether the stories are true or fabricated in order to sell more magazines. There is only one way to find out: have a talk with her beloved dog, "Tim." I decided to concentrate on a photo of this beautiful German Shepard, who passed away in 2005.

The first time I tried to speak to Tim, he told me he was

busy and couldn't talk. He politely asked me to contact him later. Sure enough, he greeted me in a couple of hours with a big smile.

**"I'm ready for you now, and I'm glad you're the person who's going to interview me," he said.**

"Why is that?"

**"Because you're an honest person and don't trash people."**

He seemed quite sincere. I blushed with the compliment and started interviewing him: "What exactly was your job? Were you Shania's companion, watchdog, or both?"

**"I kept her company and protected her because there are so many crazy people out there. That's why she wanted a big dog like me instead of a miniature one."**

"You have such a nice smile. I wonder how you could scare anybody!" I tried to sound casual.

**Tim looked at me with a twinkle in his eyes, but then suddenly he frowned and looked quite threatening. "This is what I look like when I want to scare people," he said.**

He certainly did look frightening, so I changed the subject with another question: "Did you travel with Shania or did you stay home during her tours?"

**"I went with her everywhere, of course. How could I keep an eye on her if I stayed behind?"**

He was shocked that I would suggest such a thing.

"She took good care of me during our trips. She almost spoiled me. Fortunately, I have a lot of common sense and take my job seriously."

"Please tell me more about Shania. What kind of person is she? How has fame affected her and her family?"

"Well, that's a lot of questions at the same time. Let me see what I can do. She's a vegetarian, she works hard, and she loves her family. She also loves horses and donates a lot of money to charity. She even wrote a song for charity," he said, with obvious pride in his voice.

"I know she's happy now and has a lot of money, but did she have a lot of money when she was a child?"

His mood changed, and he seemed almost sad. "She was poor when she was a child. First, her birth parents got divorced, and then her mother remarried. She loved her new dad, but there was not much money, so Shania had to sing in clubs," He paused for a moment, and then added: "When she was around 22 years old, her parents were killed in a car accident, and she had to take care of her siblings. Those were tough days. I feel so sorry for her."

I could swear the dog had tears in his eyes. "We all know Shania has sold lots of albums, but is there something you're especially proud of?" I said.

"Of course! She's an Officer in the Order of Canada. It's a great honor. She's also on the Canadian Walk of Fame, and there's a museum dedicated to her in her hometown. These are great achievements. Sooner or later she'll have a star in Hollywood!"

"Her name wasn't always 'Shania.' Why did she change it?"

"It was 'Eileen Regina,' but a few years ago she decided to follow her adoptive father's Indian heritage and chose the name 'Shania,' which means 'I'm on my way.' I like it much better than 'Eileen,'" he said.

"I agree. So what do you call her: 'Eileen' or 'Shania?'"

"I call her 'Mum,' because she's my adoptive mother," he said, adding "She takes good care of herself, exercises, and eats right. But I'll tell you a little secret: she likes hot chocolate."

This comment made me laugh. "Was it hard to leave her behind when you died?" I said.

"Oh yes, but there was nothing I could do. My time on earth was over, and I had to leave. I'm always with her in spirit, and I'll be back with her later on, perhaps when she lives in New Zealand. I've always wanted to live there."

I was surprised by this news. I had no idea Shania was thinking of living in New Zealand.

I thanked Tim for his time, and he told me to contact him again if I needed to know more.

I was impressed with this perfect 'gentledog.'"

# II

Do Famous Owners and Their Pets Get Together at the Rainbow Bridge?

Sooner or later people and pets pass on. We all hope that when it happens we will be together again with our loved ones who passed before us: our parents and grandparents, and also our uncles, aunts, cousins, siblings, and old friends.

Most of us have pets we dote on, and some people wonder if there's one heaven for people and another one for pets. Is there even a heaven at all for pets? Will pets be with their owners when they pass away? What happens if the pet dies and the owner lives a few more years? Will they meet on the other side? Can the spirits of pets come back and protect their owners? Are the owners aware of the presence of their deceased pets? And, what happens if the owner dies first? Will his or her spirit come back to be with the pets and make his or her presence known to them?

I decided to ask some pets who had belonged to famous owners what they knew about the "Rainbow Bridge," the crossing place between this world and the next.

# Audrey Hepburn &
# Mr. Famous

Most of us remember Audrey Hepburn, who was a beautiful and talented actress. She seemed to have it all: beauty, health, money, fame, and class. But was there more than the public could see? What was behind that exquisite face?

I've always been intrigued by this extraordinary woman, who won so many awards. I wanted to find out more about her. What was she really like? Was she as sweet as she looked? Had her life been as easy as it seemed? I decided to concentrate on her dog, a little Yorkshire named appropriately "Mr. Famous," because he was the closest link I could find. He was also completely unbiased and devoted to her.

Mr. Famous told me his owner, whom he affectionately called "Audy," was the most loving person in the world, and he was proud to have played in some of her movies. He told me she was compassionate, in spite of the tough times she had endured when she was a child. This surprised me, because I didn't know anything about her life. After all, I had not read gossip magazines when she was alive. I just like watching her films. So, I asked him what he meant by this remark.

He was a bit reticent about talking to me, because he had heard how the paparazzi can slander people. I assured him I wasn't a reporter, and that I was just interested in understanding their relationship. I told him I had great admiration for his "Audy."

I was able to convince him to trust me. He started telling me a lot of things that had happened to her—even before he was born. He told me about how difficult the divorce of Audy's parents had been. At the time, it was rather unusual for couples to get divorced. He also told me she had changed schools several times, and it was hard for her to leave her friends behind. Even though she had no problems making new ones, she definitely missed her old friends.

But then the worst came—Audy and her mother were living in Holland when Hitler occupied the country. I was shocked. I never suspected that behind her peaceful face there had been this kind of suffering. Mr. Famous told me

Audy had nightmares and cried in her sleep.

**"But I lick her tears and give her a kiss," he said.**

He was proud of being able to comfort her in her times of need. I could see in his eyes that he was becoming sad, so I asked him to tell me about the good times.

This cheered him up, and he started telling me about how proud he was of her achievements. He also told me her favorite colors were pink and white, but fortunately she never made him wear a pink coat. However, he didn't mind sleeping on pink cushions and, of course, he loved her ballet slippers.

"But aren't you colorblind?" I asked.

**"Well, they smell different," he said, giving me a big smile.**

I definitely could not argue with this—it had never crossed my mind that colors smelled different.

He told me Audy was afraid of horses and had fallen off one and injured herself. He also told me she was a tidy and disciplined person. He said she always smelled wonderful. Clearly, his nose must have been sensitive.

**And the funniest thing: "She didn't like champagne, but she enjoyed drinking a beer occasionally."**

It had never crossed my mind that a pet would notice something like this.

He told me they had some lovely years together, but then

he found out he would be crossing the Rainbow Bridge in a few weeks. He was sad but didn't show it, because he didn't want to spoil the time they had left together. He didn't want to make Audy unhappy.

**He also told me that even though it had been hard to leave her behind, he knew it wasn't her time yet. "Fortunately, my mother, father, grandparents, uncles, some siblings, cousins, and old friends were there to greet me and cheer me up," he said. "I really enjoy being with them again."**

It seemed as if he almost felt guilty about enjoying himself on the other side of the Rainbow Bridge.

Mr. Famous said his spirit often came back to be with Audy. He was there to greet her the day she passed, and her spirit held him as she ascended to heaven, where they've been together ever since. He felt sorry for the loved ones she left behind, but he was happy she finally could see and hear him, and hold him again. He shed a tear as he reminisced.

He went on to say that when they reincarnate he knows they'll be together again on earth. He doesn't know when this will happen but, for now, they're enjoying their stay in heaven.

# Ronald Reagan, El Alamein & Little Man

I've always been fascinated by Ronald Reagan. I wondered what he was like as an actor and as the President. Why did he leave a successful career in Hollywood to become the Governor of California? What was his marriage to Nancy Reagan like? Was she running the White House, not the President? Did Nancy really visit an astrologer? How were his relationships with his children? After all, he had been married twice and had an adopted son.

I decided to ask "El Alamein" and "Little Man," two of his

favorite horses, what Ronald Reagan was really like. El Alamein is a beautiful white horse who was a present from a Mexican president. Little Man is a gorgeous chestnut stallion. Ronald Reagan used to ride both of these horses at his ranch, the "Rancho del Cielo."

The first thing El Alamein told me was that until he came to the United States he could only speak Spanish, and he was surprised when he found out he could understand everything Ronald Reagan said to him in English. El Alamein called Ronald Reagan "Ronnie." He told me that even though he was used to mingling with presidents, he felt proud to belong to the most powerful man in the world.

I didn't need to ask any questions. Instead, he volunteered the information.

El Alamein told me he had been nervous about moving to a foreign country and getting a new owner, because nobody knows how a new owner will treat their horse. But as soon as he saw Ronald Reagan he knew he had come to the right place. Ronnie was everything an animal could hope for: strong, intelligent, kind, honest, fair, and an outstanding rider. And after all, they had been together in other lives.

He told me Ronnie always took his job seriously, whether it was acting, governing California, or being the President of the United States.

**"Ronnie used to talk to me, and we'd discuss state matters,"
El Alamein said. "Everything was confidential, but he knew I
wouldn't tell anybody, not even the people who could hear
me."**

El Alamein continued: "Sometimes it was hard for Ronnie to make decisions that might hurt people, but he always kept the interests of America above everything else. He always listened to his advisors, but ultimately it was his decision, and he certainly had to make some tough ones. Ronnie used to say, 'It certainly is lonely at the top, old friend.' I always nodded in agreement. I was happy to be there for him when he needed me."

Little Man saw Ronald Reagan in a different light. He wanted to talk about the "Gipper's" private life. At first, I had no idea who the Gipper was, but Little Man looked at me in disbelief and told me this was the name he called Ronald Reagan. I became excited about getting a different angle on the former President.

Little Man started by telling me he agreed with El Alamein about the Gipper having so many good qualities. He said: "The Gipper was an affectionate man. He loved Nancy, his children, his family, his animals, and above all, his country. He would defend it, even if it meant he had to die."

I told him I already knew about this and would appreciate some comments about the Gipper's private life.

"I'm getting there. Don't be impatient," he said, as if to scold me.

I felt like a child who has been caught with a hand in the cookie jar.

Then, Little Man told me the Gipper had a strong sense of duty towards people. This is why he had served in the Army and always regretted not having gone abroad to fight.

He also told me the Gipper had enjoyed immensely being a lifeguard for seven years.

**"It was rewarding in more ways than you think," Little Man said.**

"Oh, what do you mean?"

**He looked at me with a mischievous smile. "Well, think about all the young ladies who were impressed with the dashing lifeguard. He was never short of dates during those years!"**

I had to laugh—this horse had a sense of humor. Then he went on to say that the Gipper had a heart of gold. He had been married before and had three children by his first wife.

I was surprised to hear this. I knew he had two children, but where was the third one?

**Little Man spoke again: "Christina was premature and only lived for a few hours. The Gipper used to talk to her spirit while he was riding."**

**He paused for a moment and then continued: "Nancy was the love of his life, his soul mate, everything he wished for in a woman: smart, intelligent, vital, loving, and beautiful. She had impeccable taste and a great personality. Plus, she would stand up to her husband when she felt he was being unreasonable."**

I was rather curious about the rumors that it was Nancy Reagan who really ran the White House.

**"Nonsense," said Little Man. "Sometimes, the Gipper would**

discuss state matters with her, but after great consideration of what his advisors had told him, he would always make the final decision. They discussed things like any other couple, but he made the decisions."

"What about the astrologer?"

"Nancy did consult an astrologer, but she also knew the astrologer would only advise her on the favorable and unfavorable astrological times so they could be better prepared. In the end, Ronald and Nancy Reagan made their own decisions based on facts and realities, while also considering the astrologer's advice," said Little Man.

This made sense. "Just one last question: Was there any jealousy or competition between you and El Alamein for the Gipper's love?"

Little Man shook his head straight away and said: "No, there was enough room in the Gipper's heart for both of us and for all the other animals, too."

I was delighted to meet such wise animals, even though they had touched on such different aspects of President Reagan's life.

# Bill Clinton & Buddy

Some years ago, I was watching the news on television when I saw that somebody had given a puppy to President Clinton. He was named "Buddy." He was a cute little brown dog. I just hoped "Socks," the First Family's cat, and Buddy would get along.

Occasionally, I heard about the President and Buddy doing this or that. I never thought too much about it until the "big scandal." Then I was glad that no matter what the President might have done—or not done—he had someone who would not judge him: Buddy, his loyal dog. It can be lonely at the top, as President Reagan's horses had already told me.

I became curious. What was Buddy's relationship with the First Family like, in particular with the President? What did Buddy really think about the big scandal? What did he think about the intern who was at the center of it all?

I needed to find out, so one day I concentrated on Buddy's photo and asked him if he would talk to me.

**He scrutinized me and said: "No problem. I know you're not interested in trashing the President. You just want to know about him and his family."**

I was really impressed with the wisdom of such a young dog, and I assured him that he was absolutely right. I wasn't interested in any gossip, just what he had to say.

**"The President and I became buddies at first sight. Even though he was much older than I was, sometimes I wondered if I wasn't wiser than him. On occasion, he really behaved like a teenager. I tried to advise him—not on state affairs, which he handled very well—but on his private life. I wish I could have had a "dog to man" talk with him but, unfortunately, he was unable to hear me. It would have saved him, his family, and the country a lot of pain."**

**He continued: "I like Hillary and Chelsea, but they're more cat people than dog people. Bill is truly a dog person."**

I could almost hear the pride in his voice.

**"I loved playing ball with him and going for long walks. We had**

extensive talks, or should I say he talked a lot about everything and I listened. He shared his views on politics and his marriage, girlfriends, fears, aspirations, dreams, music, and other things. What bored me, mostly, was the politics. I never could understand why he and Hillary were so excited about it."

Buddy had much more to share: "I also worried about the way Bill ate. He loved burgers and junk food, and didn't seem to understand that it wasn't good for him. He was a grown-up man, so he had to watch what he ate. He could not carry on eating the same way he did when he was a teenager." Buddy sounded as if he was still worried about Bill's diet and health.

I thought to myself: *What an observant dog.*

Buddy went on to say: "Then there was...well, a change in the air. Bill started looking worried and unhappy. One day he told me: 'I did something silly. It's the biggest mistake of my life. I'm scared, and I hate to hurt my family, but it's inevitable. I just hope everyone will forgive me.'"

Buddy turned gloomy: "It killed me to hear the bad news, but I had the feeling this was serious and wouldn't go away. I knew I needed to give Bill even more love and affection than usual."

"Bill was absolutely right. Things got pretty ugly, and he suffered a lot with the situation. He also felt terrible about the pain he had caused his family. He even cried when we were alone together. Those were very dark days," said Buddy.

I wanted to know what Buddy thought about Monica, so I asked him.

"She was a sweet, young girl who fell madly in love with a much older man. I just wish she had never worked at the White House," said Buddy. "I think it was good we left the White House and moved on with our lives."

Buddy became serious. He said that in the autumn of 2001 he felt his time on earth was coming to an end. He also said that he wouldn't mind going to heaven, except for the biggest question: Who would watch over his beloved Bill?

"Bill is vulnerable and doesn't take good care of himself. Who will go for walks with him and listen to him? I promised myself that even if I had to leave, my spirit would come straight back to look after Bill and wait patiently until his time on earth ends and he can join me on the other side."

I was touched by Buddy's wisdom and dedication. I'm sure when it's time for the President to go to the Rainbow Bridge they'll be together again. At last, Bill Clinton will be able to see and hear his beloved dog, Buddy.

# III

## What Do Celebrity Pets Think About Their Coworkers?

We've all seen films with animal stars and enjoyed watching them perform all kinds of tricks and rescues. Everyone loves watching the whales, dolphins, and sea lions perform stunts at Marine World.

I've always wondered how they do it. It seems so easy to make these animals play whatever scene or perform whatever trick is necessary. But is it really that easy? Do the human stars who work with them really know what they're doing? Is it difficult for them to control the animals? Are they afraid of them? Do they get attached to the animals they work with? What about the actual owners or trainers? Do they get frustrated with the behavior of the human stars or even a little jealous? What do these famous pets think of their coworkers?

We're about to find out.

# Bruiser

I became curious when I was watching *Legally Blonde 2* and saw the scene with the little Chihuahua and the huge Rottweiler.

I had enjoyed watching *Legally Blonde* and thought it was adorable that Reese Witherspoon took the Chihuahua with her everywhere she went. Of course, the fact that "Bruiser" was such a small dog helped. What intrigued me the most, however, was the movie *Legally Blonde 2*, especially the scene where the huge Rottweiler falls in love with the tiny Chihuahua. What a funny scene. So I decided to ask Bruiser, the Chihuahua, what he thought about his coworkers.

Bruiser has sharp eyes, and there's very little he misses. Even though he's a big star, he isn't spoiled at all, and he has a tremendous sense of humor—as I found out during this interview. First, I asked him how he felt about being a dog-actor.

He smiled and said: "I've always known I wanted to be an actor, but there aren't any acting schools for dogs, so I learned as much from other dogs and watched as many films with pet actors as I could."

"How exciting. And how smart of you," I said. Honestly, I had never thought about an acting school for dogs.

"I never worried about my size, you know. After all, expensive things can come in small boxes."

We both burst into laughter. "So how did you feel about playing in *Legally Blonde*?" I said.

"I loved being carried around by Reese. She's such a great actress. She's also pretty, intelligent, and has a lot of common sense. I really enjoyed doing the first film and was hoping there would be another one. I was ecstatic to hear about *Legally Blonde 2*—and that I would have such an important role."

"How do you feel about wearing a skirt and all kinds of different outfits?" I said.

His demeanor turned serious: "Oh, it doesn't bother me. I'm also a model and, after all, I'm a professional."

"What did you think about the other actors and actresses in the film?"

"They were okay, even though they might act silly or mean in the film. There was nothing they could do about it. They had to play their roles. Of course, I like some people more than others, but that's normal."

"What about the gorgeous Rottweiler?" I said.

"We got along beautifully. He's a fantastic actor, well behaved, loving, and quite a ladies' dog."

He seemed pleased with himself and gave me a naughty smile.

"What do you mean by 'quite a ladies' dog?'" I asked.

"Well, you know, we were playing like we were gay, but that's not true. He absolutely loves young female dogs! He's quite a Don Juan," he said.

Thank you so much for your help," I said, and then I threw him a kiss."

# Willow

One Sunday afternoon, as I was scrolling through the television channels, I noticed a film I had never seen before. I began watching it—even though it had already started—because it featured Orlando Jones and he's funny. I was happy I had turned on the film, because the cast included an adorable little dog.

**I was surprised when the dog told me: "My name is 'Willow,' and I'm an actor."**

"Okay, but do you always talk to people when they're watching a film?"

**"Oh no," he said. "You are one of the few people I've spoken to,**

but I like you because you can hear me. It's frustrating to talk to people who can't hear animals."

"I'm flattered," I said. "But isn't it unusual for animals to talk from the screen to someone watching a film?"

"Not really. We just choose not to. Also, sometimes we like one person in the audience but not the others."

This made sense. I felt honored that Willow had chosen to communicate with me. Even though I was taken aback, I wanted to ask him some questions because he seemed so willing to talk.

"Did you always want to be an actor?" I said.

"Not really, but when I was discovered I knew it was exactly what I wanted to do. I work hard, but there are a lot of perks that come with the job. I bathe quite frequently because my fur needs to look shiny and clean. I also get manicures and pedicures. I'm given treats as a reward for my work. I also get lots of petting and cuddles, and I meet many nice people."

This dog definitely knew how to appreciate the finer things in life, and I wanted to know more. "Aren't you afraid of doing the dangerous scenes?" I said.

"Oh, I don't do those scenes. My owner would never let me do anything like that. They get other dogs to replace me."

From this I learned there are also stunt dogs, exactly like stunt humans. I had never thought about it before.

"What do you think of your fellow actors?" I said.

"I've acted in a lot of films and television shows. I liked most of the other actors. They all think I'm cute. I like Orlando Jones very much. He's very talented, and he makes me laugh. While we were filming, I talked to him and advised him about his acting. I don't think he heard me, though, because he never did anything I told him to do."

He seemed disappointed for a moment, but then he said: "I've been interviewed by Jay Leno. I'm flattered that he invited me to be on his show. I think Jay's great."

"What about Vivica Fox and Eddie Griffin?" I said.

"Eddie Griffin was okay, and Vivica was so beautiful. I hope my next girlfriend will be as beautiful as Vivica," he said, sounding hopeful.

"What about the other dogs on your team?"

"They're good workers, but I'm the leader of the pack. I also have a son who will follow in my footsteps."

He didn't say anything else after this comment. I just hope his son won't decide he doesn't like acting and choose to go in another direction. Willow would be so disappointed.

# L***assie

When I was little, my parents took me to see children's movies like *Cinderella*, *Snow White*, films with Charlie Chaplin, and, of course, Lassie. Lassie's movies were my favorites. I really enjoyed watching that brave dog rescue people and other animals, help kids find food, and do all kinds of other brave things. I was fascinated by that wonderful dog, and as soon as I came home I told my own dogs all about Lassie. They would smile at me when I asked them: "Would you do that for me?"

The answer was always the same: "We would die for you

and the rest of the family. Now tell us more about the film!"

Some years went by, and we finally got a television set. What a joy it was to watch the *Lassie* shows with the family pets. They enjoyed the episodes as much as we did. Needless to say, our imaginations started working, and we tried to repeat some of the tricks afterwards. This usually got us into trouble—some things are not supposed to be repeated in real life.

As I became older, and there were more important things to do, my thoughts of Lassie were pushed to the back of my mind. But then, one day, I turned on the television and saw that an old episode of *Lassie* was playing. I sat down to watch the show, and it brought back so many childhood memories.

I knew the dog who had played the original Lassie must be dead. There was no way that dog could still be alive, but the "Lassies" in the shows from different eras all looked the same. Were they all related or was it only an illusion?

What had Lassie's life as an actor been like? Was the dog a he or a she? Did Lassie enjoy the work and the other actors? I was curious, so I decided to look through some newspaper clippings and see if I could find an old photo. I knew I must have a clipping somewhere. Lady Luck must have been on my side, because I found a photo. I took this as a sign that I should have a talk with Lassie.

I was looking forward to finding out what this dog felt and thought about being an actor. I could hardly wait until I found the time to do it. I finally managed to sit down with the photo of Lassie and ask a few questions.

"Is Lassie really your name or was it your stage name?"

"'Lassie' was my stage name. My real name is 'Pal,' but sometimes I almost think my name really is 'Lassie.'"

"So, what should I call you, 'Pal' or 'Lassie?'"

"Since this a private talk, please call me Pal."

"I really need to ask you a question, but you might find it silly: Are you a male or a female? You play a female on the screen, but 'Pal' is masculine name."

Pal burst into laughter, and then he explained: "I'm a male, but I play a female. Don't worry about it. A lot of people think the same thing."

"Why don't they use females?"

"Well, male dogs are bigger, so we can play the role better. Also, our coats are fuller and this makes us look stronger."

"Did you always want to be an actor?"

"I didn't care what I did, as long as I could work hard. I'm a working dog."

His pride in his career was evident from his tone of voice.

"Did you like your coworkers? Did you have a good relationship with them?" I said.

"I liked most of them and, of course, some of the actors changed from time to time, but we were almost like a family. It was very funny to see myself and my stage friends in a movie," he said.

"You didn't belong to an actor or the film company, did you?"

"Oh no. I had two owners: Rudd and Frank. I loved them very much. They treated me so well...."

His voice trailed off, and for a moment he seemed nostalgic for his long-ago friends.

"What about your private life. Did you have a girlfriend?"

"Oh yes," Pal said, becoming obviously excited. "I had lots of girlfriends, and I have lots of children, grandchildren, and even great grandchildren."

"So, are they all actors?" I said.

"Some of them became actors, but we don't do films anymore. We do celebrity appearances!" he said, in his most important tone of voice.

"Do you remember the theme song for Lassie?"

"Yes. It was written by Les Baxter. I was happy when he was chosen to write it because he really had talent. Did you know that we both have stars on the Hollywood Walk of Fame?"

"No, I didn't. Are there other dogs who have stars, too?"

"I think there are two other dogs with stars," said Pal.

"Please tell me a little more about your life when you were not working."

"It was a pretty normal life: taking walks, playing, exercising, just like any other dog. I also had to go to the vet to get my shots. I had a lot of girlfriends because Rudd and Frank wanted to have a lot of my puppies. I really enjoyed that part."

He continued: "Unfortunately, I started getting older, and I knew that I would be leaving this earth soon. I was sad to leave my family and owners behind. I explained to everybody that I was going on a long trip and would be waiting for them on the other side. I also told them my spirit would be with them until the day I reincarnated. I knew this wouldn't be for a long time because I had to be on the other side of the Rainbow Bridge for Rudd when he passed away. He would need me"

Pal is such an intelligent dog. He still is in heaven with Rudd, and I wonder when he will be ready to come back to his earthly family. In the meantime, I'm sure that some of his dog-family has joined him, too.

# IV

## How Do Celebrities Acquire Their Pets? Where Should Anyone Get a Pet?

We have seen throughout this book that some celebrities have purebreds purchased from breeders or pet stores, and some have pets they've adopted from shelters. Some even have pets who just turned up at their door.

Is it terribly wrong to buy pets from stores and breeders? This depends on the circumstances. If the potential pet owner has a particular breed in mind and can't find one in a shelter, a pet will have to be found somewhere else. Also, people who like taking their pets to shows need to get them from certified, reputable breeders who will provide the necessary paperwork.

Reputable breeders don't make too much money. They just love the animals and want to see them in shows and winning prizes. They also test the animals they sell in order to make sure they're healthy, don't suffer, and won't become a financial burden for their new owners.

We have all heard about working animals, such as horses and dogs. For example, police dogs are highly trained and perform a valuable service. These dogs work very hard to help the police find drugs, bombs, and missing people. Quite often, they put their own lives at risk.

Working with the blind also requires specific breeds that must be acquired from specialized breeders. Some breeds are more suitable for certain jobs than others, so obviously the right animal should be chosen for the job.

More and more, hospitals and senior citizen homes use therapy dogs, who bring joy and delight to sick people, particularly children and the elderly. On a lighter note, dogs and pigs are used to find truffles, but only specific breeds can do this kind of work.

Unfortunately, some breeders have no scruples, standards, or respect for animals. They keep them in horrible conditions and mate them excessively in order to provide litter after litter—until the female dies of exhaustion. They only care about making money. Fortunately, society is becoming much more aware of these terrible circumstances, and these people are being caught and punished for their cruelty.

I'm always shocked when I hear about someone who decides on the spur of the moment to give a pet as a present for Christmas, a birthday, Valentine's Day, or some other occasion without considering the full consequences of such a responsibility. Sometimes, the recipient of the gift is not prepared to make the changes in his or her life that are needed to care for a pet. Occasionally, the person who receives the pet is allergic to that particular type of animal. Also, it can get quite expensive to keep a pet. Money for food, toys, equipment, and veterinary bills is required, and some people just can't afford it.

Shelters are a great place to adopt most types of animals. Of course, if you want fish, a tarantula, a snake, a turtle, a lizard, a bird, or some other exotic type of pet, it's more likely that these animals will be found in a pet store.

Adopting a pet from a shelter not only saves a life and gives an animal a good home, but shelters often have an agreement with local veterinarians. This makes it less expensive to give the animal a good start with a free medical exam and shots. Many shelters will also implant a microchip into the pet, so if it gets lost the pet can be easily found and returned to its family.

Due to the overpopulation of some animals, shelters often make arrangements with veterinarians to have the animals neutered or spayed at low cost. There are many pet shelters in the United States, the best known being The Humane Society and The Society for the Prevention of Cruelty to Animals (SPCA). These non-profit agencies can be found almost anywhere. They're quite strict about who can adopt a pet, and they try to make sure the animals go to good homes. See the resources listed at the back of this book for more information on organizations and their Web sites.

I admire celebrities who adopt pets from shelters without worrying about the animal's pedigree. These animals are as loving and caring as the ones who come from a good breeder.

# PET RESOURCES

Humane Society: *www.hsus.org*

The American Society for the Prevention of Cruelty to Animals: *www.aspca.org*

Much Love Animal Rescue LA: *www.muchlove.org*

Northshore Animal League America: *www.nsalamerica.org*

Animal Rescue on TV: *www.animalrescuetv.com*

Petfinder: *www.Petfinder.com*

Pets 911: *www.Pets911.com*

Local shelters and animal rescue groups

9 781582 701554